Reflections on the Path to Wholeness
Volume 1

A Journey of Redeeming Faith

BRENDA S. JACKSON, PH.D.

*Priority*ONE
publications
Detroit, Michigan, USA

Reflections on the Path to Wholeness: A Journey of Redeeming Faith
Copyright © 2007 Brenda S. Jackson, Ph.D.

All scripture quotations, unless otherwise indicated, taken from the HOLY BIBLE, NEW INTERNATIONAL VERSION®. NIV®. Copyright© 1973, 1978, 1984 by International Bible Society. Used by permission of Zondervan. All rights reserved.

Scripture quotations marked (KJV) are taken from the HOLY BIBLE, KING JAMES VERSION (Authorized).

All poetry submissions herein are © 2000 – 2005 Brenda S. Jackson

All rights reserved. No part of this publication may be reproduced, stored in a retrieval system, or transmitted in any form or by any means – electronic, mechanical, photocopy, recording, or any other – except for brief quotations in printed reviews, without the prior permission of the publisher.

*Priority*ONE Publications
P. O. Box 725 • Farmington, MI 48332
(800) 331-8841 Nationwide Toll Free
E-mail: info@p1pubs.com
URL: http://www.p1pubs.com

ISBN: 978-1-933972-05-X

Edited by Patricia A. Hicks
Cover and interior design by PriorityONE Publications

Printed in the United States of America

TABLE OF CONTENTS

Acknowledgements

Dedication

Preface

Seminar #1 Looking in the Mirror 13

Seminar #2 Forgiving the Unforgivable...............................35

Seminar #3 Faith – The Amen Factor....................................77

Seminar #4 A Journey With A Future *(Poetry)*.................101

About the Author 114

ACKNOWLEDGEMENTS

I acknowledge the Tuesday Morning Intercessory prayer group of New Prospect Missionary Baptist Church whose unceasing prayers brought this book to fruition.

I acknowledge Christina Dixon of PriorityONE Publications who took on a new venture in publishing a non-conventional book and spent tireless hours in producing a format with continuity.

I acknowledge the editor, Patricia A. Hicks, who changed the spoken word format to the grammatically correct written word.

I acknowledge Chaplain C. Vaughn Brown of the Robert C. Scott Regional Correctional Facility for Women and Coordinator Verleen McLemore of Camp Brighton, Michigan Correctional Facility who provided opportunities for these Christian Seminars to be provided for the inmates at these facilities.

I acknowledge my family and my Pastor, Reverend Dr. Wilma R. Johnson, who are supportive of prison ministry.

DEDICATIONS

This volume is dedicated first and foremost to my Lord and Savior Jesus Christ and second to all current and former inmates of Scott's Correctional Facility, Camp Brighton Correctional Facility, Ryan Correctional Facility, and the St. Louis Correctional Facility who participated in the seminars and facilitated seminar development by candidly expressing their needs.

In addition, this work is dedicated to all who provide service to Jesus by visiting those in prison regardless of the opposition.

PREFACE

It was in March, 1995, when Chaplain Mary Ann McCann, Chaplain for Metropolitan Jail Ministries, Wayne County Jails, invited me to be a part of the Metropolitan Jail Ministries (MJM) Re-Entry and After-Care Program. I was requested to provide six to eight hours of training in anger management for all inmates who were sentenced to at least six months at the William Dickerson Detention Facility, Hamtramck, Michigan, and to provide a similar seminar for participating volunteers. With guidance from our Lord, the help of the Christian Conciliation Council, and my training and education in conflict resolution, a seminar was developed.

From April, 1995, through March, 1997, with the assistance of Brenda Rudolph, a worker in MJM's jail ministry, and Yolitha Hill, a student in mental health completing an internship in jail ministry, weekly seminars were provided, and every inhabited "pod" was reached. This was the beginning of Christian-based seminars to the incarcerated to assist in breaking strongholds, in developing life skills, and preparing for re-entry into society, with the goal of reducing recidivism. That one seminar has increased to over 17, and various presentations have been provided at Robert C. Scott's Women's Correctional Facility in the State of Michigan, Camp Brighton Michigan Correction Facility, Indiana Women's Correctional Facility, The St. Louis Michigan Correctional Facility, and the Michigan Ryan Regional Correctional Facility.

Reflections on the Path to Wholeness is a series of seminars put in a format to enable clergy and Christian lay persons to facilitate and utilize the materials to assist them in rebuilding broken lives and providing spiritual growth to overcome life's obstacles. Anyone trapped by circumstances may receive benefit.

Each seminar is a separate document, providing broad goals and objectives, presentation materials, group exercises, personal examinations and group interactions, scriptural references, and explanations as foundations for Bible study and applications.

Volume I, *A Journey of Redeeming Faith,* has a total focus of first looking inward for change. Portions of my personal journey toward wholeness are seen in the original poems which accompany each seminar section. Poetry is another pathway toward wholeness and is encouraged.

It is my prayer that the contents of this volume, and those to come, although not necessarily unique, will be additional tools used in building the Kingdom of God right here on earth, as we prepare for the return of our Lord and Savior Jesus Christ.

Minister Brenda Simuel Jackson, Ph.D.
Author

Looking in the Mirror

SEMINAR OBJECTIVES

- Identify Positive Character Traits
- Identify Negative Character Traits
- Identify Methods of Changing the Negative Character Traits to Positive
- Identify How to Strengthen the Positive Character Traits

SCRIPTURES

James 1:23 – 25 (Amplified Version)
For if anyone only listens to the Word without obeying it and being a doer of it, he is like a man who looks carefully at his [own] natural face in a mirror;

For he thoughtfully observes himself, and then goes off and promptly forgets what he was like.

But he who looks carefully into the faultless law, the [law] of liberty, and is faithful to it and perseveres in looking into it, being not a heedless listener who forgets but an active doer [who obeys], he shall be blessed in his doing (his life of obedience).

Matthew 5:3-9

Blessed are the poor in spirit, for theirs is the kingdom of heaven.

Blessed are those who mourn, for they will be comforted.

Blessed are the meek, for they will inherit the earth.

Blessed are those who hunger and thirst for righteousness, for they will be filled.

Blessed are the merciful, for they will be shown mercy.

Blessed are the pure in heart, for they will see God.

Blessed are the peacemakers, for they will be called sons of God.

DOWN A DARK TUNNEL
© Brenda Simuel Jackson

1996, one year left of seminary, and it started.
Somebody's been through my desk, I thought.
Where are the checks with scripture, I just bought.
Is someone following me that I cannot see?
Oh, Lord what is happening to me?

He sat next to me, and brought my eyes on a bullet to gaze,
He then said, your car could go up in a blaze.
Oh Lord, I thought in dismay.
Over my shoulder I began to constantly look,
Waiting for that deadly hook.

1997, graduating in six months.
The class met at the airport ready to go,
I couldn't wait I believed from this trip, I would
Mentally learn and spiritually grow.

In a foreign land we came, and fear not hope crept into my brain.
Will I be left in this place without a real friend?
Will I be shot as part of Satan's plot?
Oh Lord, don't leave me now, it is only to you I bow.

Back home again,
I brought charges against my church, my employer, my seminary,
Family and friends, all because of what I believed I had seen.
Fear was my morning call, Oh Lord You are my all.

Forced medical leave by my employer was the action.
Worker's Comp. was my reluctant reaction.
While continuing to distrust and look over my shoulder, and
Obtain my seminary degree; I heard a voice say talk to me.

Twice a month for a little while, the doctor and I talked, she always had a smile, but this talk did not quiet my fears, and I recognized the battle I was in was real. Oh Lord, help me, I know You will Win.

1997 changed to 1998, a light, Oh so small, I began to see, when the Lord said again, you must follow and lean on me. Over my shoulder, I no longer looked, and fears were conquered through reading His Book.

The struggle continues from battle to battle, but in my Lord, I know Who matters.

There is light at the end of the tunnel, and Jesus is that light who brought me through by His might.

TRIBUTE TO THE WOMEN OF SCOTT'S
© Brenda Simuel Jackson

You have the mind of Christ,
    You know how to do that which is right.
You have the mind of Christ,
    You know how to live in order to be blessed.
You have the mind of Christ,
    Your intentions are good.
You have the mind of Christ,
    Provide good counsel to family, friend, and foe.
You have the mind of Christ,
    Know that God will order your steps.
You have the mind of Christ,
    Know that your transformation is ever growing.
You have the mind of Christ,
    Just believe in Him and show it.

My Character Traits

Seen through the Mirror of Someone Else

Request someone with whom you have interacted on several occasions to complete this character portrait of you by checking those items which mirror your character traits.

__ Ambitious	__ Gentle
__ Powerful	__ Weak
__ Controlling	__ Meek
__ Popular	__ Sad
__ Quiet Spirit	__ Merciful
__ Happy Personality	__ Mean Spirited
__ Self-righteous	__ Unconcerned
__ Righteous	__ Hateful
__ Fearful	__ Trustworthy
__ Intelligent	__ Reliable
__ Wise	__ Critical
__ Hostile	__ Judging
__ Malicious	__ Nurturing
__ Loving	__ Accepting
__ Rational	__ Impartial

List five traits checked that I wish to change:

1. _____
2. _____
3. _____
4. _____
5. _____

List five traits checked that I wish to strengthen:

1. _____
2. _____
3. _____
4. _____
5. _____

My goal is to achieve change by (date:) _____

THE INNER PERSON

Matthew 5:3

I. **Poor in Spirit – An Attitude of Dependence**

    A. Poor – πτωχοσ
    B. Need of God's grace
    C. Dependence on a greater power
    D. Not a state of material poverty

II. **A Dependent Relationship with Christ**

    A. Know we exist because of the sacrifice of Jesus Christ
    B. Know in whom to trust
    C. Know we share in the salvation of God
    D. Have humility

THEREFORE

Psalm 1

    A. Do not allow self to be advised by the wicked
    B. Do not associate with those whose life is only sin
    C. Do not take on ways of those who are against God
    D. Meditate on God's Word
    E. Obey His Word

CHARACTER TRAITS

- Quality of being approved
- Test to determine genuineness
- Develop over time through trials
- Attitude resulting from faith (James 1:2-4)
- Result of relationship with Christ (Matthew 5:3-7:28)
- Show by one's conduct

Finish each of these sentences:

1. When I am on detail, I show my dependence on Jesus when _____.

2. When I am given a ticket which I believe to be unfair, I demonstrate my dependence by _____.

3. When I have successfully completed three months without giving in to the urge to smoke, I know my dependence is not on self but _____.

4. In times of frustration, I _____.

5. When making choices, I will depend on _____.

CONFESSION OF TRUST

Psalm 121: 1, 2, 4

Speaker #1: I lift up my eyes to the hills [hills around Jerusalem], where does my help come from?

Speaker #2: My help comes from the Lord, the maker of heaven and earth!

Speaker #3: (Jeremiah 3:23) Truly in vain is the hope of salvation from the hills and from the tumult and noisy throng on the mountain; truly in and with the Lord our God rests the salvation of Israel.

Speaker #2: He will not allow your foot to slip or to be moved; He who keeps you will not slumber.

III.   The Character of Mourning – An Attitude of Sadness
    A. πενθεω = grieving outwardly, sadness
    B. Know that sadness should be temporary
    C. Why do we mourn
        1. Sin of self
        2. Sin of others
        3. Loss
    D. Reasons why sadness is temporary
        1. If we have Jesus, there is joy (Matthew 9:15)
        2. God is comfort (2 Corinthian 1:3)
        3. The enemy of death has been defeated (1 Corinthian 15:21)
    E. Seek the comfort that is available
        1. Encouragement (1 Corinthian 14:3)
            a. Sins forgiven
            b. 1 John 2:1
        2. Seek assistance (John 14:16, Romans 1:12)

IV. **Attitude of Meekness**
   A. Synonyms in Ephesians 4:2 AMP
      - Lowliness of mind (Humility)
      - Unselfishness
      - Gentleness
      - Mildness
      - Patience
   B. Meekness is Power
      - Jesus The Christ – Non-violence; love
      - Martin Luther King – Non-violence
      - Billy Graham – Never a political entity
      - Mother Theresa – Giving, humble
      - Rev. Dr. Wilma R. Johnson - Joy
   C. Gaining in Meekness
      - Be not arrogant in accomplishments
      - Share your gifts
      - Use kind words
      - Guard what you say

V. **Attitude of Righteousness**
   A. Righteousness is not anger between self and brother (Matthew 5:21-2)
   B. Righteousness is not lust which leads to adultery in the mind (Matthew 5:27-30)
   C. Righteousness is not seeking retaliation (Romans 12:17)
   D. Righteousness is justice and equity (Leviticus 19:15)
   E. Righteousness is being lawful (Genesis 7:1)
   F. Righteousness is being morally clean (Exodus 9:27)
   G. Righteousness is equity of character (Matthew 3:15)
   H. Righteousness is equitable action (Romans 2:26)

GENERAL CHARACTERISTICS OF RIGHTEOUS LIVING

(Book of Proverbs)

- Does not cheat (10:2; 23:10)
- Works for a living (10:5)
- Has a good reputation (10:7)
- Is diligent (12:27)
- Provides for the needy (14:31)
- Searches for evidence and the correct way (14:14; 25:8-9)
- Doesn't listen to lies and/or gossip (17:4)
- Doesn't rejoice at calamity (17:5)
- Has security in God's Word (18:10)
- Listens before speaking (18:13)
- Chooses friends wisely (18:24; 27:9-10)
- Lives discretely (19:11)
- Accepts discipline (19:20)
- Doesn't get intoxicated (20:1)
- Is a good strategist/planner (20:18)
- Hides from evil (22:3)
- Doesn't chase wealth (23:4)
- Disciplines children with love (23:12-14)
- Ministers to his/her enemies (25:20-22)
- Is humble and not boastful (27:1-2)

MERCY INDEX
Answer each statement truthfully about yourself.

True   False

                I am one who can easily ignore one in need.

                I have compassion if it doesn't hurt.

                People must earn my favor.

                Mercy is only a sympathetic emotion.

                Mercy is a response to a need for help.

                I am merciful.

VI. Attitude of Mercy – Attitude Toward Those in Distress
Galatians 6:16

A. Mercy is love which knows no rank.
- Reaches out to meet need without considering the merit of the person
- Atonement, a place of propitiation
- Prayer – cry for mercy (Psalm 6:9, 86:6)
- Compassion
- Mercy is to show favor, kindness to an inferior
- Merciful is being moved to help
- Jesus encouraged others to have mercy, "Be merciful, just as your Father is merciful." (Luke 6:36)

- "…Those who share God's heart will identify with the needy and show solidarity with the oppressed." (NIV Encyclopedia, 440.)

VII. **The Character of a Pure Heart**

   A. Matthew 5:8, the Greek word for pure (although an adjective) is one of continuous action of being cleansed
      1. A **pure** heart shows love (1 Timothy 1:5)
      2. A **pure** heart has a clear conscience (1 Timothy 3:9)
      3. A **pure** heart is sincere in faith (Hebrew 10:22)
      4. **Pure** is being genuine (Philippians 1:10)
      5. **Pure** is being chaste and holy (Philippians 4:8)
      6. **Pure** is being free from sin
      7. **Pure** is being guiltless

   B. The heart represents the unity of spiritual, physical and mental being (NIV Encyclopedia, 334)
      1. The Center of the will, and intellect of the mind (Genesis 6:5)
      2. The soul of the person (Ephesians 6:6)
      3. The heart expresses the inner life
      4. The heart can be corrupted:
         a. Jeremiah 17:9-10 The heart is deceitful above all things and it is exceedingly perverse and corrupt, and mortally sick
         b. The heart represents the hidden but true aspects of one's life
         c. 1 Peter 3:4, But let it be inward adorning and beauty of the hidden person of the heart with the incorruptible and unfading charm of a gentle and peaceful spirit.

NEED A HEART CHECK?

Matthew 5:13-43

- Un-reconciled Relations?
- Lustful Eye?
- Sinful Hand?
- Swearing Oaths?
- Retaliating Punch?
- Unwilling to be pressed into service?
- Works do not praise God?

How pure is your heart?

VIII. The Attitude of a Peace Maker

    A. Peace signifies wholeness, and the Hebraic term has been translated as salvation.

The verb to make peace is to bring about reconciliation.

שָׁלֵם, shalom means: wholeness, unity, harmony,

Shalom conveys concept of prosperity, health, fulfillment

SCRIPTURE	DEFINITION	RESULTS OF PEACEMAKING
Genesis 29:6;37:14	Good health and wellbeing	Jacob is seeking the good health of his brother; Jacob is seeking the safety of his sons
Ezekiel 13:16 ff	Prosperity and completeness	Reconciliation with God, true prophets; The Lord is warning Israel through Ezekiel of the results of False Prophets
Job 15:21 Proverbs 3:2	Prosperity	Job's state of being before the attack of Satan. The State of man before marauders attack Describes a state of peace as long life
Isaiah 54:10	Covenant Relationship	Peace with God; No War; Human relationship
Genesis 26:26-31	Safety and welfare	International harmony; Isaac and the men of Abimelech fellowship and make an oath of peace

II. **Peace is harmonious relationships**
    i. ειρηνη - Peace with God through Christ
    ii. Symbolizes joy resulting from forgiveness
    iii. Hostility replaced by unity

iv. Colossian 3:15 Let the peace of Christ rule in your hearts, since as members of one body you were called to peace.

SCRIPTURE	DEFINITION	RESULTS
Acts 7:26 Romans 14:19	Harmonious relations	Moses tried to bring reconciliation; mutual edification
Luke 14:31-32; Revelations 6:4	Lack of hostility	Peace between nations; power
Acts 15:33; 1 Corinthian 16:11	Blessing	Friendliness among members of the council; A blessing for Timothy;
Matthew 10:13	Rest and Contentment	If as an emissary of Christ, you are welcome then bless with peace, if not keep your peace
Acts 10:36 Ephesians 2:17	Results of the Gospel	Harmonized relationships between God and man - accomplished through the gospel

III. Peace is a state of Mind
    i. Peace is a state of security
    ii. Peace is a state of order
    iii. Peace is freedom from disquieting thoughts
    iv. Peace is freedom from oppressing emotions
    v. Peace is a state of mutual accord

II. Peace is a spiritual state
   i. Peace is reconciliation to God
   ii. Peace is inner harmony [with self] possible through a personal relationship with Christ
   iii. Peace is interpersonal relationships with others made possible through the work of the Holy Spirit in us

III. Peace is a physical state
   i. Peace is having safe passage through the favor of God
   ii. Peace is being released from bondage through the actions of God
   iii. Peace is good health
   iv. Peace is good welfare

BLUE PRINT TO A PEACEFUL NATURE

- True Faith in Jesus Christ, accepting the peace offering He made in reconciling us back to God
- Follow the examples of Christ and the Scriptures:
  - Act in love
  - Focus on the good
  - Practice behavior which demonstrates inner peace
  - Practice behavior which demonstrates trust by not judging, but helping one to overcome
  - Practice behavior which includes being a good listener and controlling what we say to each other
- Communicate with God in prayer
- Communicate with God in praise
- Communicate with God in thanksgiving.
- Edify the Lord in all that is done.

NOW, LOOK IN THE MIRROR, WHOSE PORTRAIT DO YOU SEE? CHRISTLY? WORLDLY?

REFERENCES

Bibles

Baker, Kenneth. General Ed. *The NIV Study Bible.* Grand Rapids: Zondervan Corp., 1985.

Radmacher, Earl D., Allen, Ronald, House, Wayne H. Eds. *The Nelson Study Bible, NKJV.* Nashville: Thomas Nelson Publishers, 1997.

Siewert, Frances, Ed. *The Holy Bible, Amplified Version.* Grand Rapids: Zondervan Corp., 1987.

Books

Richards, Lawrence O. *New International Encyclopedia of Bible Words Based on the NIV and the NASB.* Grand Rapids: Zondervan Publishing House, 1991.

The Revell Bible Dictionary. New Jersey: Fleming H. Revell Co., 1990.

Vine, W.E.; Unger, Merrill F.; & White, Williams, Eds. *Complete Expository Dictionary of Old and New Testament Words.* Nashville: Thomas Nelson Publishers, 1985.

Forgiving the Unforgivable

"Forgive us our debts, as we also have forgiven our debtors."

Matthew 6:12

SEMINAR OBJECTIVES

- To Gain an Understanding of the Various Circumstances Which Create the Need to Forgive and/or Be Forgiven
- To Understand the Spiritual, Physical, and Psychological Benefits of Forgiveness
- To Aid Participants in Disclosing Issues of Hidden Shame (Spiritual, Physical, and Psychological), and to Receive Forgiveness

MY CHILD, THE BLESSING
© Brenda Simuel Jackson

Oh Lord,
1961 was the year of a blessing,
Although I treated him like a curse.
He was healthy and strong, and
had done no wrong.
A loving mother and father who had not given birth,
took him home, they were so filled with mirth.
Years passed by, and my blessing I still had not seen,
and You Lord said go and search the scene.
Although fear of rejection and non-forgiveness filled my heart,
You sent me Lord on this journey and said do not depart.
2003, July the time of being blessed again,
coming face to face with my son in spite of my fain
The road of getting acquainted has not been all joy and laughter,
at times it has been hurtful, and felt like disaster.
But God You are in control;
You led me down this path for a reason,
Lord help me to know and trust my blessing
during this our season.

FORGIVING IS NOT EASY TO DO
© Brenda Simuel Jackson

Forgiving is not easy to do.
I was robbed of my innocence, forgiving is not easy to do.
I passed the test, surpassed qualification, but the one selected was of a lighter hue, forgiving is not easy to do.
I tried so hard, studied long, wrote the best I could, someone else got the prize, forgiving is not easy to do.
The names were harsh, the sticks large, there was no love to abound, forgiving is hard to do.
Then I remembered He who for me took this and much much more, then forgiving became easier to do.

WHAT MAY CAUSE THE NEED FOR FORGIVENESS

SCRIPTURES	CONTEXT	DEFINITIONS
Genesis 2:9	Tree of knowledge of good and evil is in the middle of the garden. Adam and Eve must make a choice between good and evil.	The Hebrew term Evil has the meaning of bad as in adversity or as in affliction. Choices may lead to a need for forgiveness.
Genesis 44:5	The use of inspiration from demons.	Evil (Hebrew language), is defined as wicked actions. Evil is to make something good for nothing.
Job 24:21	Job is describing those that God judges as wicked.	The Hebrew term for evil is defined as wicked actions, preying on the barren and the childless.
Psalm 49:5	The Psalmist describes the results of "wicked deceivers".	In this context evil has the meaning in the Hebrew of being without profit, worthlessness, the destruction often connected to ungodly persons.
Proverbs 12:21	The Old Testament belief that only the wicked have trouble.	Evil is defined as calamity, the coming to naught, or to come to vain.
Isaiah 1:16	Isaiah is telling Judah of their rebelliousness.	Evil is defined as the acts of men that mar, or cause "badness".
Matthew 5:37	Vows should not be made. Let your yes be yes and your no be no. Anything more than that comes from evil.	Evil is defined as hurtful with painful calamities.
Matthew 24:48	The true character of a wicked servant is seen when the master is absent.	The Greek term of evil means depraved, or one with a wicked character.

Mark 3:4	Jesus is asking the question of doing good or evil on the Sabbath.	Evil is described as ignoring the opportunity to do good in favor of ritual.
2 Corinthians 6:8	Paul describes his hardships	Evil is seen as being a deceiver, an imposter, or one who defames another.
Ephesians 4:31	Paul describes bitter speech.	Evil is described as evil age.
		Speaking, railing, scurrilous speech against a person; it is slander, a curse, blasphemous language.
Titus 2:8	Paul is telling Timothy to show integrity and soundness of speech.	Evil is defined as foulness.

EVIL:

Moral evil is cruelty.

Metaphysical evil is blindness.

Physical evil is an earthquake. (Geisler, Norman, 333)

Evil is not a thing, but it is a real lack in things.

Evil is not nothing; it is the lack of something. (Ibid)

Evil is a corruption of something. Evil cannot exist on it own, but good can. (Ibid)

EXISTENCE OF EVIL

I. God created the possibility for evil to exist because He gave man free will.

II. Evil is not caused by God, but the freedom to sin causes evil.

III. Evil is anything that frustrates human aspirations and expectations.

FILL IN THE BLANK:

Evil is _____ .
Evil is _____ .
Evil is _____ .
Evil is _____ .
Evil is _____ .
Evil is _____ .

PROBABLE ANSWERS:

Evil is pain.
Evil is disease.
Evil is hate.
Evil is murder.
Evil is cruelty.
Evil is corruption.
Evil is sickness.

Read Matthew 18:21-35
Discuss the evil motives or results of the actions mentioned.

BEHAVIOR REQUIRING FORGIVENESS

SCRIPTURE	BEHAVIOR	ACTS OF FORGIVENESS	CHASTISEMENT /MERCY
Genesis 3:1-21	Adam and Eve disobeyed God, Eve submitted to deception	God made the atoning sacrifice and clothed their nakedness.	God made the way for reconciliation to Himself and the ground was cursed, woman given pain in child bearing, and they were put out of the garden of Eden.
2 Samuel 11:1 – 12:22	David lusted, committed adultery and murder, and caused the enemies of God to show contempt.	The Lord took away David's sin.	The son of the sin did not survive.
Hosea 1:1 – 3:5[1]	Gomer, the wife of Hosea committed prostitution, adultery, and abandoned her husband and family.	Hosea sought his wife, bought her out of slavery and prostitution.	Reconciliation of Hosea and Gomer

---

[1] Note this is a type of Israel as the wife of God, demonstrating the unfaithfulness of Israel.

SCRIPTURE	BEHAVIOR	ACTS OF FORGIVENESS	CHASTISEMENT /MERCY
Jonah 2:1 – 2:10	Jonah was disobedient to the Lord's command to preach deliverance to Ninevah.	Jonah, in the act of drowning inside the belly of the big fish, was kept alive.	Jonah was given a second chance to obey God.
John 8:3-11	A woman (and man) was caught in the act of adultery.	None of the elders, teachers, etc. could carry out the sentence of the law, stoning; no one could condemn the woman.	Jesus forgave, and did not condemn her.
Mark 15:27; Luke 23:39-42	A robber	Jesus answered his cry for eternal life.	Crucified, given a place in heaven.
Acts 7:54 – 8:1; 9:1-31	Paul who threatened the people of the Way, put believers in jail, and did nothing to stop the stoning of Stephen.	Met Jesus after His ascension, forgiven, and given a mission for Christ.	Apostle to the Gentiles; martyred in Rome.

ACTS OF UNFORGIVENESS

SCRIPTURE	CONTEXT	ACTS OF UNFORGIVENESS	THE UNFORGIVER	RESULTS	FUTURE FORGIVING RESULTS
Genesis 27:2, 41 Genesis 33:11	Isaac, the receiver of God's covenant promise, is preparing for future death and tells the eldest, Esau, to prepare a meal so he can eat and then give him his blessing.[1]	Through deception, Jacob received the blessing reserved for the first born, Esau, who would be responsible for caring for the family after Isaac's death.[2]	Esau	Esau held a grudge against Jacob because of the blessing his father had given Jacob. His words, "The days of mourning for my father are near, then I will kill Jacob. Genesis 27:41 Jacob had to flee causing family separation.	Jacob humbled himself and 14 years later returned to his homeland, and Esau forgave him, bringing about reconciliation.
Genesis 39:19	Joseph is a slave in Potiphar's house. He was in charge of all that Potiphar owned. He was trusted. Joseph was well-built and handsome, and Potiphar's wife lusted for Joseph and wanted intercourse.	Joseph refused the advances of the wife and when she attempted to physically capture him he literally ran out of his clothes (tunic or cloak).	Potiphar's Wife Potiphar	Joseph was jailed and remained in jail for two years for doing that which was right.	

[1] Note: A blessing is the method of passing on any family wealth.
[2] Note: This was God's divine Will, that Jacob would receive the blessing.

ACTS OF UNFORGIVENESS

Judges 19:18-25; 20:6- 21:1	A Levite was traveling with his concubine and servant and going toward home through the land of the Benjamites. He sought and accepted the hospitality of a resident to spend the night as it was getting dark.	"Wicked persons" who wanted to have sex with the Levite, took the Levites concubine and raped and abused her until she died.	The Levite	The Levite cut up the body of his concubine, and sent a piece to each tribe of Israel. The tribes demanded that the guilty parties be handed over, and this was refused. This led to war against the Benjamites. Over 50,000 people died, the town was burned, and the tribe cut off from the rest of the tribes.	Restoration through worship and providing wives to the Benjamites.
2 Samuel 13:7 – 18:9	Amnon, David's son, is in love with his half sister, Tamara and desires to have sex with her.	Amnon tricks David and Tamara to get Tamara alone in his bed chambers. When she refuses his advances, he rapes her and then discards her leaving her in disgrace. David takes no action against Amnon.	Absalom	Absalom becomes bitter, and plots for two years, and kills Amnon, after which he is forced to flee Jerusalem. When David allows Absalom to return, Absalom conspires against his father, taking the Kingdom, and causing war. Absalom is killed by David's commander.	

ACTS OF UNFORGIVENESS

		The rape is told to Absalom, Tamar's brother.		
Jonah 1:1 – 4:3	Ninevah, the capital of Assyria, had in early years destroyed Samaria, the capital of Israel (Northern Kingdom), defeated Judah, and humiliated Jerusalem through harassment and exploitation. Ninevah was seen as merciless against the Jews. Jonah was told by God to go and preach to this people who had shown no mercy against his people. Jonah ran not wanting Ninevah to be given an opportunity for forgiveness and salvation, and not face judgment.	The repentance of Ninevah and the delay of God's judgment.[3]	Jonah	Jonah was angry and asked twice that God take his life, he could not accept that God forgave Ninevah.[4]

---

[3] Note: The scriptures describe the repentance of Ninevah and states they believed that God would judge them.

[4] Note: After 100 years, Ninevah returns to old behaviors, and God's judgment is executed. Nahum 1:1–3:19.

Divorce

(Among Believers)

Purposes:

- To set forth circumstances which permit legal divorce under the law
- To define adultery
- To set forth that an alternate to marriage is celibacy
- To describe the divine nature of marriage

Argument: Divorce is not within God's Divine Will

Marriage is ordained by God. Divorce is not similarly ordained. Separation is allowed with the concept that reconciliation is possible. During periods of separation, the parties are to be celibate. Even in situations where a spouse is a non-believer, the believer should not leave the marital situation, but is not expected to prevent the non-believer from leaving should the same occur. Divorce is not given as an option for the believer.

Under permissive law, divorce is permitted when the wife [or husband] is believed to have committed immoral acts. Remarriage may be permitted under these circumstances.
However a just partner cannot remarry an unjust partner. The general "guideline" is to practice celibacy and to remain unmarried if divorce for other than immoral acts should occur.

O.T. VIEW DIVORCE	Deuteronomy 24:1-4	N.T. VIEW Matthew 5:31-32	Matthew 19:3-12	Mark 10:1-12	1 Corinthians 7:10-16
Circumstances	Wife is found to be immoral	Wife is found unchaste	Moses permits, if wife is immoral	Moses	Partner is a non-believer
Consequences	Husband sends wife away; gives a certificate of divorce	Husband sends wife away and gives bill of divorce	Disobedience to God's Word	Disobedience to God's command and His Word.	The unbeliever may voluntarily leave; celibacy
God's View	A divorced woman is defiled; God's Will does not include divorce.	Permitted, if woman unchaste	Not lawful; be celibate	Not permitted	Should not leave the unbeliever; become celibate
Remarriage	None	Will cause adultery	Allowed only if divorce was result of immorality.	If either party remarries, commits adultery	Do not remarry.

EXODUS AND THE ABORTION ISSUE

EXODUS 21-22: ANALYSIS AND LOGIC

I.   Context:

21:20 relates to how man treats slaves, and verse 26-25 relates to how man treats his servants. Verse 22 has emphasis on the husband's possession, a wife. The immediate context of verses 20-21, and 26-27 clearly relate to possessions of the man. The key object is therefore harm to the husband's possessions, child and wife.

The dispute in verse 22, is between men, not between the wife and a man, or a wife and her husband (NASB). The hitting of the wife is (probably) accidental, although scripture does not clearly state this, it is implied. The hitting is therefore "unintentional". The context provides for differences in judgments for intentional and non-intentional crimes. (21:12,21:28-29, 35-36)

If the wife "aborts, gives birth prematurely (NKJV, Scofield), or miscarries (NASB, Thompson Chain), the damage is punishable through the same forms of judgment as similar crimes, restitution, redemption, etc. If there is further injury, then "life for life" is the punishment. (see 21:12)

The questions remain: 1. Did the wife give premature birth to a live baby, or did she miscarry/abort a dead child? 2. Does further injury refer to the baby, the mother, or both? The context implies that the reference is to both as death to either is further loss to the Husband. The reference says "life for life, eye for eye, tooth for tooth …" implying that a loss is a loss. Scripture indicates the importance of an heir for the preservation of Israel, children are a blessing, and obedience provides for this blessing from God. (23:26)

II. Key Word:

The Hebrew word to denote action of aborting or miscarrying in verse 22 has the meaning of something born. The term is rooted in the meaning of to bear, to beget. The NASB uses a term meaning "to come out anytime," and is rooted in the same word as in verse 22. In Hosea 9:14, the term, SHAKOL is used to indicate an action of making barren, to suffer abortion or be made childless. This is not the term used in v. 22 of Exodus 21. The NKJV uses a term ALAB which has several uses but indicates that the fruit is gone or is departed. Based on word usage, it can be concluded that this situation is a premature birth. Therefore, further injury is probably death.

III. Remaining Question:

If the woman is struck before the fetus can be born alive and she miscarries, could further injury only relate to the wife? Would the deliverance of a dead fetus be a case of a "life for a life"? Although contextual analysis and the analysis of the above key word do not provide a clear answer, it is clear that the fetus is a life.

SECRETS OF SHAME
NEVER DIVULGED, NEVER FORGOTTEN

Following is a list of shameful occurrences in one's life that may have never been shared with anyone, possibly not even God, although He knows.

Check those that apply to you which you can now openly disclose to God and to one other person of trust.

- ❑ Sexually fondled as a child/youth by a relative/family friend, and no one was ever told.
- ❑ Approached by a person called of God for sexual favors.
- ❑ Stole goods from a retail outlet.
- ❑ Lied and caused personal harm to others.
- ❑ Used illegal drugs.
- ❑ Was/Is a closet alcoholic.
- ❑ Fired for legitimate reasons.
- ❑ Participated in illicit sexual activity.
- ❑ Abused physically/sexually/psychologically another person.
- ❑ A victim of abuse.
- ❑ Other _____ .

WHAT IS SCRIPTURAL SHAME?

I. Old Testament
בּוֹשׁ - (bos)
- evil doer
- sexual immorality
- nakedness
- indecent things
- things impure
- uncleanness

II. New Testament
ατιμια - (attimia)
ασχημσυνη - (aschemosune)
- Vile passions
- Dishonor
- Nakedness
- Deeds of darkness
- Dishonest gain

III. <u>Shame</u> in Scripture is normally an issue of morality, and/or sexual conduct.
    A. Undisclosed behavior
    B. Leads to emotional grief/guilt
    C. There is a loss of innocence

SCRIPTURAL ISSUES OF SHAME

Scriptural Context	Issues of Shame and Current Application	Removal of Shame
Genesis 2:7-11 Adam and Eve were naked in the garden with no shame. They are in moral innocence with eyes of righteousness until they become disobedient.	Nakedness is an euphemism used to connote a form of sexual behavior. With the loss of innocence came the emotion of shame. They were able to see each other's sexuality from a lustful, shameful view. Application: The shame we felt when we lost our innocence and did a deliberate act of sin against the knowledge of God.	Acknowledgment to God and receiving His covering.
Genesis 9:22-23 Ham saw the drunkenness and nakedness of his father Noah.	Nakedness is sexual activity. To uncover a person's nakedness is to participate in sexual activity; to see one's nakedness is to see some form of sexual activity, such as indecent exposure, or nocturnal emissions. Ham saw some form of sexual indecency about his father.[2] Application: The shame of indecent exposure, seen or as a participant.	1. Disclosure of the sin 2. Having the sin covered 3. Putting the incident behind 4. Obtaining forgiveness

---

[2] Some commentators *(The Bible Knowledge Commentators),* believe it was Ham who had relations with his father, sodomy, but the Hebraic form is self reflexive in v. 21 and the term uncovered is not used. The text should be literal, that Ham saw. Other Commentators put stress on the drunken condition of Noah as the real nakedness or shame. (Matthew Henry)

Leviticus 18:6-18: Prohibitions against all forms of incest 2 Corinthians 2:5-11 Restoration of one accused of incest	Sexual behavior with a family member as recorded in 1 Corinthians 5:1. Application: Undisclosed knowledge of or participation in such activity	- Confession - Repentance - Accept forgiveness - Accept (any) punishment - Put it behind
Deuteronomy 23:12-14: Handling of bodily excrement	God is not to be in an unclean place. A place is designated outside of the camp where one is to relieve oneself. Then one is to dig a hole and cover it up. Failure to do this is to invite God into an unclean place. Application: When/if we get to a point in life that we lose control over our elimination function, there is shame and feelings of being unclean.	Matthew 15:11, lets us know it is what we say that will make us unclean; it is disobedience that will make us unclean. Spiritually we are clean; the body is what is decaying.
Deuteronomy 25:11: If two men are fighting, and the wife seeks to rescue her spouse, she grabs the opponent by his private parts.	The knowledge of the private parts of one who is not one's spouse should bring shame. Application: Your only knowledge of someone's sexual parts should be your own spouse.	Old Testament requires punishment, but we can turn to 1 John 1:9. Jesus will forgive.

Scriptural Context	Issues of Shame and Application	Loss of Shame
Isaiah 1:29 Shame resulting from sexual immorality at Pagan sites.	Application: illicit sexual activity	1 John 1:9; 2 Corinthians 7:1 Confess Repent Receive purification separate self from activity
Isaiah 54:4 Plight of widowhood	Shame of rejection by one's spouse, and the shame of widowhood. Application: Guilt of singleness	Turn to God
Ephesians 5:11-12 Undisclosed sin; Deeds of darkness	Application: Believers are to expose sins, even the sins of others. There is shame when we turn away or ignore the truth. Such samples include persons living together without marriage, hidden adultery, and hidden fornication.	Ephesians 5: 12-14 Expose it (not to the public) Don't dwell on it Pray

Keys to Cover all Shame and Guilt:
Hebrew 1:3, 9:14 – Purified by the blood of Christ.
Acts 15:9 – Our hearts are purified through faith.

HANDLING THE GRIEF OF SHAME

1. Open Disclosure: Share, confess the event(s), share the pain of the shame, and express the guilt. (Prayer of forgiveness)

2. Know beyond any doubt that Jesus forgives. Do not deny that the situation existed, and do not intellectualize the event(s), which will cause a reoccurrence of denial.

3. Express anger, remorse, and disappointment that the event happened. This may be directed to God who promised to keep you from falling, and not to put more on you than you could bear.

4. Be honest with self about choices made, and recognize that any discipline is because God loves you.

5. Read Scriptures, put your faith in God's Word to ensure escape from any future situations, contentment with present circumstances, and a growing testimony of your strength through Jesus to overcome.

6. Understand why you were weak, know now that your strength is not of yourself, and know that God is not the reason for the past hidden shame. Prayer for God's continued strength and praise Him for releasing you from guilt.

7. Continuously give praise to God, with thanks for your spiritual discipline and release.

8. Journal how you feel about yourself.

SCRIPTURES AGAINST LUST OF THE FLESH

Romans 13:12-14
The night is nearly over; the day is almost here. So let us put aside the deeds of darkness and put on the armor of light. Let us behave decently, as in the daytime, not in orgies and drunkenness, not in sexual immorality and debauchery, not in dissension and jealousy. Rather, clothe yourselves with the Lord Jesus Christ, and do not think about how to gratify the desires of the sinful nature.

1 Corinthians 6:13b-20:
The body is not meant for sexual immorality, but for the Lord, and the Lord for the Body. By his power God raised the Lord from the dead, and he will raise us also. Do you not know that your bodies are members of Christ himself? Shall I then take the members of Christ and unite them with a prostitute? Never! Do you not know that he who unites himself with a prostitute is one with her in body? For it is said, "The two will become one flesh." But he who unites himself with the Lord is one with Him in spirit. Flee from sexual immorality. All other sins a man commits are outside his body, but he who sins sexually sins against his own body. Do you not know that your body is a temple of the Holy Spirit, who is in you, whom you have received from God? You are not your own; you were bought at a price. Therefore honor God with your body.

1 Corinthian 7:2
But since there is so much immorality, each man should have his own wife, and each woman her own husband.

Galatians 5:19
The acts of the sinful nature are obvious: sexual immorality, impurity and debauchery.

Ephesians 5:3-4
But among you there must not be even a hint of sexual immorality, or of any kind of impurity, or of greed, because these are improper for God's holy people. Nor should there be obscenity, foolish talk or coarse joking which are out of place, but rather thanksgiving.

THE DIVINE GIFT

I. Typology of Forgiveness
   A. Definitions
      1. Old Testament terms for forgiveness were connected with sacrifice.
         a. כפף is to cover (Leviticus 16)
         b. To appease (sacrifice)
         c. Make atonement (sacrifice)
         d. נשא in Genesis 50:17, Psalm 4:6 means to cast away.
            i. To lift
            ii. To carry
         e. Forgiveness offers pardon to sinners (Psalm 32: 1-5)
      2. New Testament forgiving is receiving unmerited favor.
         a. αφιημι, in Matthew 18:21-27, a conversation between Jesus and Peter on the number of times to forgive, and Jesus' parable compares forgiveness to settling accounts
            i. To send forth
            ii. To send away
            iii. To remit
            iv. To settle debts
         b. A derivative of the Greek word to forgive has the meaning of debt
         c. In Aramaic the term used for debt is the same as the term used for sins
         d. Matthew 9:2, 5, 6, sins are completely blotted out
         e. Luke 6:37, the term forgive means to release or to dismiss
         f. 1 Peter 4:8, the term forgive means to remove from sight

B. The Relationship of forgiveness and Salvation (Romans 5:9, 15-18; 8:15-17; John 3:16-17; Ephesians 2:7)
1. Salvation is the work of God to release man from sinful state.
2. Salvation releases man from the judgment of eternal damnation.
3. Salvation is being rescued.
4. The process of forgiveness (a part of Salvation)

Scripture	Old Testament	Scripture	New Testament
Leviticus 16:7-10³, 20-21, 4:1-21	**Atonement** for sin, burnt offering, and the scape goat	Hebrew 12:1-3; 2 Corinthians 5:21; Philippians 2:6-8	**Jesus** is our atonement; through Jesus there is forgiveness of sins.
Genesis 48:16	**Redemption** is to deliver from harm.	1 Corinthians 6:20; 7:23; Revelation 5:9	**Jesus** purchased us from sin, released us from the debt of sin, and has given us an inheritance.
Leviticus 6:30; 8:15	**Reconciliation** is offering of a blood sacrifice on the altar for atonement.	Romans 5:10-11, Colossians 1:19-23	**Jesus** through His death reconciled the believer back to God.
Leviticus 4:32-35	**A Propitiation (an appeasement, sacrifice)** is offered to the Lord by the **High Priest**.	Hebrew 2:17-18	**Jesus** is our appeasement and High Priest.

Leviticus 16:7 depicts two goats. One goat is killed and offered, and the second goat is a scape goat on which the sins are symbolically placed and the goat is sent away. This is an antitype which means a counterpart of Christ in the New Testament.

Leviticus 6: 5-7	**Trespass** offerings for **forgiveness**.	Ephesians 2:13-16	**Jesus** committed the legal act of removing charges and the debt owed, and giving peace and unity.
		Acts 13:39	**Jesus'** righteousness is imputed to the believer. The believer is declared righteous.

C. Divine forgiveness is received through belief in Jesus Christ.
 1. God provides the forgiveness.
 2. Man believes in the Gospel of Jesus Christ
 3. Man confesses Christ, repents of sins.
D. The need for Divine forgiveness is not from the actions of man.
 1. The universality of sin is the result of Adam's disobedience to God. (Roman 5:12, 16, 19, Galatians 3:10, Ephesians 2:1-3)
 2. Man has an innate sin nature. (Psalm 51:5; Romans 8:21)
E. Blessings of Divine Forgiveness bring Freedom. (Psalm 32: 1-2, 5-6)
 1. Our sins are covered.
    a. Freedom
    b. Declared righteous
 2. Iniquity is not imputed to us.
    a. Clean Slate
    b. Full Pardon
 3. In us there is no deceit
    a. Inward honesty
    b. Honesty toward God
    c. Honesty toward man

F. There is a continuing need for Forgiveness (1 John 1:6-9; Ps 32: 3-4)
   1. There is anguish when we do not seek forgiveness.
      a. The body worries
      b. The body produces stress
      c. The body holds anger
      d. The body becomes bitter
   2. The Lord is against those who do not seek forgiveness.
      a. The guilt cannot be hidden
      b. We are separated from His protection
      c. Our fellowship with God is disrupted
   3. We have no strength when we keep our sins hidden
      a. The strength is used keeping the secret
      b. We can't use the strength of Jesus to ward off other sins

HUMAN FORGIVING

I. Concept of forgiveness
   A. Christian creed based on the ethical character of God. (Ephesians 1:7)
      1. Jesus turned away God's wrath.
      2. Christ atoned, covered our sin. (Ephesians 2:3; John 2:2, 4:10)
   B. Biblically, Christians are to forgive. (Matthew 6:12)
   C. Forgiveness is a gift given to someone who has harmed you.
   D. Union between Spirit and Forgiveness changes a person. (Joanna North)
      1. Recognition that human being is more than material.
      2. Forgiveness is a therapy which may transcend any denominational belief system. (North, p. 17)
   E. The ability to forgive indicates the capacity for moral actions.
      1. The new creation of the believer. (2 Corinthian 5:17)
      2. Fruit of the Spirit. (Galatians 5:22-23)
   F. Forgiveness is a voluntary act.
      1. Forgiveness does not negate a wrong act.
      2. Forgiveness is a release from a wrong act.
      3. Forgiveness is the cancellation of a debt.
      4. Forgiveness is a suspension of a deserved penalty. (Vines, p. 251)
   G. Forgiveness is an emotional action.
      1. Forgiveness is abandoning one's angry feelings.
      2. Forgiveness is abandoning one's angry thoughts.
      3. Forgiveness is giving up the wish to punish.
      4. Forgiveness is giving up the desire for revenge.
      5. Forgiveness replaces negative cognitions with positive cognitions.

      H. To forgive is to give someone else life. (Prodigal Son, Luke 15:11-32)
      I. Human Forgiveness is not reconciliation.
          1. Forgiveness happens on the inside. (Worthington, 129)
          2. Reconciliation is within a relationship.
          3. Reconciliation is not always the "safe" avenue. (Worthington, 130)

II. There is an impact on the person who is unable to forgive and to reconcile. (Ibid.)
      A. Mental Reactions
          1. Revenge seeking
          2. Retaliation
      B. Seek social justice
      C. Try to move on with life accepting the hurt
      D. Verbally saying I forgive, while internally retaining the unforgiveness
      E. Constant thoughts of the offender (p. 117)
      F. Stress responses exist
          1. Automatic reaction of stress occurs when see the person.
          2. Seek to withdraw from the person
              a. Unable to withdraw emotionally
              b. Unable to withdraw mentally
      G. Depression
      H. Fear leading to all effort to avoid. (p. 115)
      I. Physical effects also occur. (Worthington, 120)
          1. Muscle tension
          2. Viscera (Pounding heart)
          3. Neurochemical stimulation of the brain

III. The impact of not forgiving is the same as the impact of not seeking forgiveness. (1 John 1:6-9, Psalm 32:3-9)
    A.   There is anguish when we do not seek forgiveness.
        1. The Body worries.
        2. The body produces stress
        3. The body hold anger
        4. The body becomes bitter.
    B.   Persons can defend against giving forgiveness.

"Those who psychodynamically defend against giving forgiveness will not experience a great amount of emotional anguish. (Worthington, 117)
        1. Little anger
        2. Little hatred
        3. Little desire for revenge

IV. Persons are more likely to give genuine forgiveness if there is justice.
    A. Justice is exacting a penalty.
        1. The Lord (Romans 12:19)
            a. Unrighteousness results in God's righteousness (Romans 3:5)
            b. Deuteronomy 32:35 "It is mine to avenge, I will repay. In due time, their foot will slip."
            c. Vengeance meets with salvation
            d. Redemption meets with salvation (Isaiah 61:1-2, 63:4)
            e. Biblical concept of justice includes divine retribution (2 Thessalonians 1:6-9)
        2. The Law
            a. Divine Law
            b. Civil Law
    B.   Forgiveness does not replace justice.

V. The results of forgiving
   A. Rev. Everett's forgiving the person who killed his son started to heal (The Detroit News, Dec. 21, 1997)
   B. Roman's 8:28 in Action. "For the Love of Prisoners" by Noel Piper
   C. Alleviation of distress (Worthington, 139)
   D. Alleviation of low self-esteem (Ibid)
   E. Reduces urge to retaliate (p 108)
   F. Increases pursuit of conciliation if moral norms can be re-established
   G. Compassion replaces anger
   H. Degree of sadness lessened
   I. Hopelessness is lessened
   J. Despair is lessened

BALANCE SHEET FOR FORGIVENESS[4]

Can You Forgive?

Check The Following Statements you can agree with:

- ___ Vengeance is not mine, but God's.

- ___ Retribution is not mine, but God's.

- ___ Forgiveness allows me to detach myself from a person's inappropriateness.

- ___ Forgiveness gives me freedom.

- ___ Forgiveness pleases God because it allows Him to fill me with His character.

- ___ An unwillingness to forgive only creates imprisonment.

- ___An unwillingness to forgive will cause me to be like the one I disrespect.

- ___ I can choose to hold a grudge.

- ___ Forgiveness is not obligatory.

- ___ My other relationships are enhanced when I am willing to forgive.

---

[4] Minirth & Carter, 217.

PROCESSES OF FORGIVING

WORTHINGTON:

1. Ensure that the person understands forgiveness (review the Comparison of what is and is not forgiveness)
2. Obtain a commitment to try to forgive.
3. Get a partner to assist:
   a. Express the event
   b. Describe the thoughts
   c. Describe your feelings (p. 119)
   d. Together feel the hurt
4. Describe your feelings when you think of the person you have not forgiven.
5. Empathize with the one who hurt you.
   a. Understand the offender
   b. Seek to show compassion
   c. Exercise anger control
6. Offer Forgiveness
7. Make a verbal commitment to forgive
8. Write a certificate stating the date of forgiveness
9. Write a letter of forgiveness explicitly forgiving the person from whom harm was received.
10. Read the letter aloud confidently to a trusted confident to a trusted confident, if none, Jesus is the best.
11. Pray over sending the letter.
12. Send the letter as prompted by Holy Spirit.
13. Maintain a journal of thoughts (if any), regarding the offender.

PROCESSES OF FORGIVING

SCHMIDT PROCESS: (Schmidt, Doug, "The Prayer of Revenge", Helping People Forgive The Unforgivable." *Christian Counseling Today, 2003 11(2) 44-46.)*

Strengthen emotional confidence in God's willingness to accomplish justice.
- Deuteronomy 32:35 "It is mine to avenge; I will repay. In due time their day of disaster is near and their doom reaches upon."
- 2 Corinthian 5: 8-10 (The forgiven and the redeemed)
- Deuteronomy 32:43: "Rejoice, O nations, with his people, for he will avenge the blood of his servants; he will take vengeance on his enemies and make atonement for his land and people."
- Rev. 2011-15 White Throne Judgment

Interview Process:
1. What did this person do to you that created a loss for you, damaged your reputation, or cause you pain?
2. If I were to ask you to forgive this person, what would you say?
3. Is it safe for you to confront this person?
4. If it is, have you done it?
5. On a scale of one to ten, with ten (10) being genuine repentance and one (1) being remorseless, blame shifting, where would the offender land?
6. Do you expect to have a relationship with this person?
7. Will you become more vulnerable because of what this person might do if you confront them?

8. Are you confident this person, if he/she remains remorseless will one day meet God's discipline? Use a scale of one to ten with one being no confidence.

9. Have you accomplished for yourself the type of acknowledgement and acceptance of responsibility you'd like see from this person?

10. What obstacle does God need to move in this case that you cannot move?

11. Take this obstacle to God in prayer.

12. Can you now forgive the person?

PROCESSES OF FORGIVING

PRAYER

1. Admit harbor feelings of anger, hurt Psalm 4:4, Ephesians 4:26
2. Choose to forgive the person as Christ forgave us (1 Peter 2:21-25)
3. Pray: Lord help me to look at this person from your point of view, to love with your love (Romans 5:5,8)
4. Make a Commitment to God to forgive
5. Ask God to help you abandon revenge
6. Thank God for forgiving you (Romans 4:7-8)
7. Pray Romans 8:28-29, Philippians 4:8
8. Pray for the person, preferably with a pray partner. (Luke 6:28-35)
9. Admit any anger with God for letting the events occur, and ask forgiveness
10. Determine not to dwell on the past hurts
11. Let God's love rule
12. Journal every time a negative thought of the person reappears, and go through the steps again

BIBLIOGRAPHY

BIBLES

Baker, Kenneth. General Ed. *The NIV Study Bible.* Grand Rapids; Zondervan Corp., 1985.

Radmacher, Earl D.; Allen, Ronald; House, Wayne H. Eds. *The Nelson Study Bible, NKJV.* Nashville: Thomas Nelson Publishers, 1997.

Scofield, C.I. Ed. *The New Scofield Study Bible, NKJV.* Nashville: Thomas Nelson Publishers, 1967.

Siewert, Frances, Ed. *The Holy Bible, Amplified Version.* Grand Rapids; Zondervan Corp., 1987.

Thompson, Frank Charles, Ed. *The Thompson Chain-Reference Bible. NASB.* Indianapolis, Indiana: Kirkbride Bible Co., 1983.

Lexicons and Dictionaries

Arndt, William F. & Gingrich, F. Wilbur. *A Greek-English Lexicon of the New Testament and Other Early Christian Literature.* Chicago: The University of Chicago Press, 1958.

Brown, Francis; Driver, S.R.; & Briggs, C.A. *Hebrew and English Lexicon of the Old Testament.* Oxford:Clarendon Press, 1951.

Vine, W.E.; Unger, Merrill F.; & White, William, Eds. *Vine's Complete Expository Dictionary of Old and New Testament Words.* Nashville: Thomas Nelson Publishers, 1985.

Books

Enright, Robert D. and North, Joanna. Eds. *Exploring Forgiveness.* USA: University of Wisconsin, Press, 1998.

Carter, Les, Ph.D. and Minirth, Frank, M.D. *The Choosing To Forgive Workbook.* Nashville: Thomas Nelson, 1997.

McMinn, Mark R & Phillips, Timothy. *Care For The Soul, Exploring the Intersection of Psychology & Theology.* Illinois: Intervarsity Press, 2001.

Wood, Julia T. *Interpersonal Communication Everyday Encounters.* 3rd ed. Wadsworth Learning Institute, 2002.

Worthington, Jr. Everett L. *Dimensions of Forgiveness, Psychological Research & Theological Perspectives.* Templeton, 1997.

Journals and Newspapers

Piper, Noel. "For The Love of Prisoners," *Decision*, October, 2003, 32-35.

" Simple Act Became Pathway To Healing", *The Detroit News*, December 21, 1997, Associated Press.

Schmidt, Doug "The Prayer of Revenge, Helping People Forgive the Unforgivable," *Christian Counseling Today*, 11(2), 2003, 44-46.

Faith

The Amen Factor

Theme Scriptures:　　　Hebrews 11:1-40
　　　　　　　　　　　　James 1:2-8
　　　　　　　　　　　　John 3:15
　　　　　　　　　　　　 Psalm 89:1-4

SEMINAR OBJECTIVES

- Provide an Understanding of the Main Aspects of Biblical and Divine Faith
- Provide Mechanism to Recognize the Power of Faith
- Provide Understanding of How to Exercise Faith in Today's World
- Compare the Victorious Faith of Ancient Saints with the Victorious Faith of Present Day Saints
- Research and the "Faith Factor"

"MY FAITH"
© Brenda Simuel Jackson

My Lord, thank you for my faith that lets me know You are.

Thank You for my faith that changed my life.

Thank You for my faith that Jesus, The Christ, is my Lord.

Thank You for my faith letting me know I am Yours.

Thank You for my faith and its healing power.

Thank You for my faith and its strength of a strong tower.

Thank You for my faith knowing my sins are forgiven.

Thank You for my faith in knowing I have a future of eternal living.

RECOGNIZING THE CALL
© Brenda Simuel Jackson

525 Clinton Street, the place of the Old County Jail, Division II.
The place where I recognized God's call, and was told, it is True.
The basement where service was held that Sunday afternoon,
Was only bright because of the souls that filled the room.
The out of tune piano, no one could play, but we sang with gusto anyway.

My sermon, Jesus is The Light, was short and sweet, one soul said yes, and I did weep.

A road called to travel, I continue on to this day.
Jesus is the light who can be seen night or day.

Presentation and Background Notes:

Analytical Word Study of Faith:

I. Lexical Definitions:
   A. Old Testament: אָמַן (aman)
      1. The root term (the basis from which other forms of the word are derived), is defined as a term applying to God, Himself, and is "firmness, or truth", an attribute of God.[5] The Hebrew is often translated as faithfulness. The term when applied to man is also rendered faithfulness and is a derivative from the attribute of God.
      2. A second definition of the root term is a verb meaning to nourish, to be firm, to be established, to be true, to build up or to support. The definition also describes the term as a parent or nurse who fosters.[6] The term means to be firm, to be established, or to be true.[7]
   B. The English dictionary defines Faith as "allegiance, loyalty, fidelity to one's promises; belief and trust in and loyalty to God; firm belief when there is no proof.[8]
   C. New Testament: πιστευω (pisteneu) is the base verb root form meaning to give credit, to have a mental persuasion.[9]

---

[5] Harris R. Laird, ed. et al. *Theological Wordbook of The Old Testament, Vol. 1*, Chicago: Moody Press, 1980, 51.
[6] Millard J. Erickson, *Christian Theology*, Grand Rapids: Baker Book House, 1985, 938.
[7] James Strong, "A Concise Dictionary of The Words in The Hebrew Bible," *The Exhaustive Concordance of The Bible*, Mass: Hendrickson, 14.
[8] *Webster's Seventh New Collegiate Dictionary*, Massachusetts, G & C Merriam Co., 1967, 299-300.
[9] Wesley Perschbacher, (ed), *The New Analytical Greek Lexicon*. Mass.: Hendrickson, 1990, 329 and this definition is not used in the Gospels, and only once in 1 John, a different form of the word is used from *A Greek-English Lexicon of the New Testament and Other Early Christian Literature*, Eds. Williams Arndt & Wilbur Gingrich, end ed. Chicago: University of Chicago Press, 1958, 660.

D. Participants complete the first part of assessment of how they define faith.
1. Compare with partner
2. Discuss why they selected what was selected

Comment: The first aspect of the word faith combining the Old and the New Testaments is that a foundation has been created. The key elements through the root definition is that faith is predicated on the firmness of the **source** which answers the question, "why faith," the answer is God. Our ability to have faith is because of the source. It is noted we have not defined the term yet from God as the object of faith, but only as a source. A working definition of faith as "our parent, true and firm," speaks to my spirit.

II. Etymological Aspects:
The term translated from other historical and ancient near eastern languages, Akkadian, Ugaritic, and Phoenician defines faith as: to trust, and to believe.[10]
Historically in other groups, the term has been an action term indicated by the infinitive "to".

---

[10] W.E. Vine, Merrill F. Unger, & William White, Jr., *Vine's Complete Expository Dictionary of Old and New Testament Words.* New York: Thomas Nelson Publishers, 1985, 76.

III. Derivatives and Scriptural Context

DERIVATIVES OF THE ROOT אָמַן	DEFINITIONS[11]
(omen) אֹמֶן	Faithfulness
(amen) אָמֵן	verily, truly, amen
('omman) אָמָן	steady-handed
(emin) אֱמִן	Faithful, trusting
(omna) אָמְנָה	bringing up, nourishment
(eimina) אֱמוּנָה	firmness, fidelity, steadiness
(amana) אֲמָנָה	faith, support, sure, certain
(umnan) מְבָס	verily, indeed
(emet) אֱמֶה	firmness, truth
(amon) אָמוֹן	architect

The term "Amen", which we often use, evolved from this Hebrew term into the New Testament. It is an affirmation of what has been said. Notice how Paul ends many of his epistles - Hebrews 13:25, Philemon 25, and Titus 3:15. It is a term of faith.

---

[11] TWOT, Ibid.

Scripture	Derivative forms	Translation & definitions of Faith/Faithful	Scriptural Context
Proverbs 27:6	a. באמבום	To trust, to confirm, faithful (NIV, NASB)	Words of wisdom which confirm a true friend - "wounds from a friend can be trusted"
Isaiah 22:23	b. בְּעָמָבוּה	To be made firm, sure (NIV)	The establishment of God's servant as a sure "peg driven into a secure place"
2 Chronicles 20:20	c. הזמיבו	To believe, to confirm, success, established (NIV, NKJV)	Jehoshaphat encourages Judah to have faith in God and be confirmed (successful)
Deuteronomy 7:9	d. אמן	To confirm, to support (NKJV)	God is faithful in His promises for generations to come
Numbers 11:12 & Ruth 4:16	e. אמבה	To nourish (NKJV)	God is as a nurse caring for His child; Naomi becomes a nurse to Obed, the father of Jesse, the father of David
2 Kings 18:16	f. אמבלה	Pillars which support the door (NKJV)	Refers to the pillars of the Temple of the Lord.
Lamentations 4:5	g. אמכבים	Nurtured	Describes the grief for those once nurtured as royalty but now have lost support
Isaiah 25:1	h. אֱמוּבָהאָמֶן	Perfect faithfulness	Praising God for Deliverance

Scripture	Root Term	Translation (NIV, NKJV)	Scripture Context
James 2:19	a. πιστευω	to believe	James compares man's ability to believe with that of demons.
Matthew 8:13	b. πιστευω	to give credit	The genuine belief of the Centurion which resulted in a healing
2 Corinthians 5:7	c. πιστισ	firm persuasion	Walking by faith, not by sight is Paul's description of Christian confidence.
2 Timothy 2:2	d. πιστοσ	faithful	Characteristic which enables one to teach of Jesus to others.
2 Timothy 3:14	e. πιστοω	to be assured	Having assurance in your teacher from whom the Gospel was learned.

Comment: Faith is an assurance of being confirmed by knowing we are supported by Him who is faithful. Faith is defined by Kierkegaard as "being an obedient response to the word of God. …[Faith is] a correlation to God's revelation.[12]

---

[12] Bernard Ramm, *A Handbook of Contemporary Theology*, Grand Rapids: William B Eerdmans Publishing, 48-49.

INVENTORY OF FAITH PART II & III
Review of personal exercising of Faith

IV. The Power of faith is being controlled by the Word of God.[13]
 A. The power of faith is the voluntary belief in the Word of God.
  1. II Timothy 3:15-16, "…you have known the Holy Scriptures, which are able to make you wise for salvation through faith which is in Christ Jesus. All Scripture is given by inspiration of God, and is profitable for doctrine, for reproof, for correction, for instruction…" NKJV
  2. II Peter 1:20-21, "knowing this first, that no prophecy of Scripture is of any private interpretation, for prophecy never came by the will of man, but holy men of God spoke as they were moved by the Holy Spirit." NKJV
 B. The Bible is the Word of God. [14] (Mark 7:13; Roman 10:17)
 C. The Bible is the revelation or true knowledge from God.
  1. God's Word reveals who God is (Acts 14:14-17; Romans 1:18-21, Psalm 19:1-6)
  2. This revelation is the Word, spoken or written, ρημα, rhema or word, different from the "Word," Christ or λογοσ, of John 1:1.
  3. The Bible contains the "Promises" of God.
  4. Keen describes the Word as the "Voice of the Holy Spirit speaking to our hearts."[15]
 D. The power of faith is the author and fulfillment (finisher) of the Word.
  1. The Word originated with God.
  2. The Word was fulfilled by God. (Hebrews 12:2)
  3. Hebrews 11:6 tells us that without faith, it is impossible to please God.

---

[13] Ibid., 9.
[14] Samuel Ashton Keen, "Faith Papers", in *The Ages Digital Library Theology*, Albany: Book For The Ages, Ages Software, 1997, 14.
[15] Ibid, 14.

a. Anyone who comes to Him must believe that He exists.
   b. Anyone who comes to Him must believe that He rewards those who earnestly seek Him.
  4. The Bible provides the evidence of the Lord's help in the time of physical/spiritual distress. (Matthew 8:10-13, 9:2, 29)
   a. The power is the confidence that God/Christ is in the position to help us out of distress. (Matthew 9:28, Mark 11:23)
   b. He that believes on the Son of God has power, it is a conscious realization of salvation.
E. Doubt robs the power of faith. (James 1:2-8)
  1. What ever we need from God, we are to ask in faith without doubting. (James 1:6)
  2. A doubting person is an unstable person (James 1:6b)
  3. Doubting leads to confusion.
  4. The word double-minded means "two souled" or having two minds.
   a. Seeking to apply reason to God.
   b. Inability to have simple faith.
  5. Doubt (απορεω), means to be without a way. (Jesus is the Way) John 14:6
  6. Doubt is to be without resources
   a. God will supply all our needs (Matthew 6:25-33)
   b. Through Jesus Christ, we have strength (Philippians 4:13)
F. Faith and wisdom go hand in hand. (James 1:5)
  1. God gives each of us a measure of faith, we cannot let doubt cause confusion in our lives.
  2. We cannot let the lies of Satan and the world cause us to be uncertain.

       a. Sample lie: "You are only as good as what you do,"[16]
       b. Sample lie: "Working Moms are the source of all family problems!"
       c. Scripture teaches do all things as unto the Lord, (Ephesians 6:5-8)
       d. Scripture indicates that there are benefits to the family, not just financial, from the working Mom. (Proverb 31)
           i. Focus on ways in which your work has provided a positive stimulus for your family.
           ii. Remember being a good parent is not defined by if you are at home, it is what you are doing when you are home.[17]
   3. Not exercising our faith will block the assistance that God gives us.
   4. We have the assurance of answered prayers. (1 John 5)

G. The power of faith:
   1. Faith results in stability in Jesus Christ.
   2. Faith results in stability in His wisdom to sustain us through all situations.
   3. The power of faith is the confidence to lean on and trust in the Lord, with all your heart and mind, and not to rely on our own insight and finite understanding. (Proverbs 3:5)
   4. Doubt leads to discouragement, Faith gives hope. (Romans 4:18-21)

---

[16] Chris Thurman, *The Lies We Believe,* Nashville: Thomas Nelson Publisher, 1989, 64-66.

[17] See Miriam Neff, *Working MOMS,* Colorado Springs: Navpress, 1992.

V. It is our source of faith, our object of faith, and our confirmation (conviction) of faith that leads us into prayer, direct communication with God.
   A. In prayer, the statements are of certainty, "In all things (realities), with prayer and thanksgiving make your wishes known." (Philippians 4:6)
      1. God already knows.
      2. He who is above time has already executed His promise.
      3. With Thanksgiving and patience, we wait for the revelation.
   B. God commands us to use the power of prayer.
      1. Studies report the results of intercessory prayer and the power of a Therapeutic Touch.[18]
      2. Among cardiac patients there were positive results.
         a. fewer congestive heart failures
         b. fewer cardiac arrests
         c. less pneumonia
      3. Hall and Chamberlain reported studies which demonstrated that prayer was a manager of pain. (p. 49)
      4. Hall and Chamberlain reported that prayer relieved stress.
   C. Have you exercised your Faith recently? (Group Demonstration)
   D. Rewards of Faith:
      1. Everlasting life (John 3:16)
      2. Peace (Romans 5:1, Philippians 4:7)
      3. Assurance (Philippians 4:6)
      4. Rest in Christ in knowing salvation is complete (Hebrews 4:1)
      5. Joy (1 Peter 1:8)
      6. Power (Hebrews 11:33-34)
      7. Defense against the enemy (1 Thessalonians 5:8; 1 Timothy 1:19; 6:12; Hebrews 10:22).

---

[18] Benson, p 182.

      8. Good fruit (Colossians 1:4, 10)
      9. Good character (Galatians 5:22-26)
     10. Faith provides a bold witness[19]
         a. Faith results in good works (Titus 3:8; James 2:14-17)
         b. Faith drives away fear (Mark 5:36)
         c. Faith gives Victory (Galatians 2:20)
         d. Faith provides bodily healing (Matthew 9:22, 29, James 5:14, 15)

VI: Group Exercise: Building Faith Blocks to approach "The Throne of Grace."[20]

VII. Prayer Time

---

[19] In Faith Papers, Lockyer.
[20] Based on *The Lies We Believe Workbook*, Ibid. 254 - 255.

BUILDING BLOCKS[21]

1. You Are a Special Creation of God.
   Therefore:

2. You Are of Infinite Value to God.
   Therefore:

3. You Have Been Adopted by God.
   Therefore:

4. You Are a Child of God.
   Therefore:

5. You are a Brother or Sister to Jesus.
   Therefore:

6. You Are a Joint Heir with Christ.
   Therefore:

7. You Have the Holy Spirit as a Guarantee of Your Inheritance.
   Therefore:

8. You Have Jesus' Righteousness.
   Therefore:

---

[21] Adapted from *The Lies We Believe Workbook*, p. 257-259.

9. You Will Never Be Condemned by God.
   Therefore:

10. You Have Unique God-Given Abilities.
    Therefore:

11. You Can Confidently Ask God for Unearned Help.
    Therefore:

Inventory:
In each of the following situations which you have experienced, write one or two of the first actions you took immediately following the incidents.

1. Laid-off or fired from a position.
   _____
   _____

2. Placed in jail/prison.
   _____
   _____

3. Waiting for a job interview.
   _____
   _____

4. Car stolen.
   _____
   _____

5. Given an assignment to do which you had never done, and success was important.
   _____
   _____

6. Waiting for surgery.
   _____
   _____

Were your actions/reactions evidence of your faith?

APPENDIX A
Hebrews 11

Hebrews 11:1 says, "Now faith is the substance of things hoped for, the evidence of things not seen. (KJV) The Greek term, used in this context, for faith is πιοστισ, a derivative of the root for faith meaning to prove or to convince, and according to Vines, it results in an conviction based upon hearing (p. 222). Verse 1 describes the results of exercising faith, but does not define faith. Exercising faith proves, and will make real what is unseen. The NIV translation says, "Now faith is being sure of what we hope for and certain of what we do not see." Faith says Christ is returning for His Church, and exercising that faith causes one to act in a way that says YES, Christ is coming back for us. Faith is the substance, nature, of reality. The results of exercising faith understands and knowing that God said, "Let there...," and there was.

Those who exercised faith were obedient to God's Word and His Will. Examples of such are outlined in Chapter 11 of Hebrews. Abel exercised faith by being obedient through his sacrifices. Enoch exercised faith by being obedient in his testimony to God. Noah expressed faith by being obedient in building an ark, although it had never rained. Abraham exercised faith by leaving a known home land, and going to an unknown land to become the Father of Nations.

The exercise of faith goes beyond Scriptural history. Reverend Jesse Jackson, with faith interceded for 13 imprisoned Hebrews in Iran and they were released on June 11, 1999. His intercessions went beyond known religious roles, but included religious teachers, community activists, as well as rabbis. Coretta Scott King is depicted as an exerciser of faith in World Traveler, April 2002, when Jane Ammerson described how she continued to work for learning to respect others different than ourselves even in the setting of a martyred spouse.

Hebrew 11:33 helps to explain that faith is a causal factor, which has a real, genuine effect. Studies at Duke University Center for the Study of Religious, Spirituality, and Health support this observation.[22] The studies were completed in 1998 and reported that depressed patients who had a strong intrinsic religious faith recovered over 70% faster than those without strong faith. Studies by Koenig[23] and others, demonstrated that persons, alcoholics, who prayed or studied the Bible, had less relapse in six months.

Herbert Benson, M.D. provides a physical definition as opposed to a theological definition of faith. "Faith is a belief in God dispatched by our brains and is deeply soothing to our bodies."[24] The Benson definition is used in his approach to aid healing through relaxation and calmness in the body.

According to studies by Chamberlain and Hall [25] faith gave the believer comfort and consolation.

The facilitator is encouraged to search for incidents in today's environment, and exercises which demonstrate the reality (physical, not virtual) of faith.

---

[22] Koenig, H.G.; George, L.K.; Meador, K.G.; Blazer, D.G;. & Ford, S.M. "Religious Coping and Depression in Elderly Medically Hospitalized Men," *American Journal of Psychiatry,*149, 1693-1700.

[23] Koenig, H.G., George L.K., Peterson B.L. (1998) "Religiosity and Remission of Depression in Medically Ill Older Patients"' Ibid., 155(4), 536.

[24] Benson MD, Herbert, *Timeless Healing, The Power and Biology of Belief.* New York: Fireside, 1997.

[25] Chamberlain, Theodore J. and Hall, Christopher A., *Realized Religion, Research on the Relationship Between Religion and Health,* Templeton Foundation, 2001.

REFERENCES

Bibles

Aland, Barbara, et al Eds. *The Greek New Testament.* Deutsche Bibelgesellschaft: United Bible Societies, 1994.

Barker, Kenneth, et al. Eds. *The NIV Study Bible.* Grand Rapids: Zondervan Corp., 1985

Elliger, K., Rudolph, W. Eds. *Biblia Hebraica Stuttgartensia.* Germany: Deutsche Bibelgesellschaft, Stuttgart. 1967/77.

Radamacher, Earl Th.D., Allen, Ronald B. Th.D. and House, H. Wayne, Th.D. J.D., Eds. *The Nelson Study Bible, NKJV.* Nashville: Thomas Nelson Publishers, 1997.

Scofield, C.I., Ed. *The New Scofield Study Bible, NKJV.* Nashville: Thomas Nelson Publishers, 1967.

Lexicons and Dictionaries

Arndt, William F. and Gingrich, Wilbur F. Eds. *A Greek-English Lexicon of The New Testament and Other Early Christian Literature.* Chicago: The University of Chicago Press, 1984.

Brown, Francis, Driver, S.R., and Briggs, C. A. *Hebrew and English Lexicon of The Old Testament.* Oxford: Clarendon Press, 1930.

Perschbacker, Wesley J. Ed. *The New Analytical Greek Lexicon.* Massachusetts: Hendrickson Publisher, 1990.

Strong, James. Ed. *The Exhaustive Concordance of The Bible with Dictionaries of The Hebrew and Greek Words.* Massachusetts: Hendrickson Publishers.

Vine, W.E. , Unger, Merrill F., and White Jr., Williams. Eds. *Vine's Complete Expository Dictionary of Old and New Testament Words.* Nashville: Thomas Nelson Publishers, 1985.

Webster's Seventh New Collegiate Dictionary. Springfield, Mass.: G&C Merriam Co. Publishers, 1967.

Books

Benson, M.D., Herbert. *Timeless Healing, The Power and Biology of Belief.* New York: Fireside, 1997.

Chamberlain, Theodore J. and Hall, Christopher A. *Realized Religion.* Philadelphia: Templeton Foundation Press, 2000.

Erickson, Millard J. *Christian Theology.* Grand Rapids: Baker Book House, 1985.

Harris, R. Laird, Archer, Gleason L., Waltke, Bruce K. Eds. *Theological Wordbook of the Old Testament. Vol. I & II.* Chicago: Moody Press, 1980.

Neff, Miriam. *Working MOMS.* Colorado: Navpress, 1992.

Ramm, Bernard. *A Handbook of Contemporary Theology.* Grand Rapids: William Eerdmans Publishing.

Thurman, Chris. *The Lies We Believe Workbook.* Nashville: Thomas Nelson Publishers, 1995.

Journals and Computer Programs

Helm, H., Hays, J.C., Flint, E., Koenig., H.G., "Effect of Religious Activity on Mortality of Elderly Disabled and Non disabled Adults," *Journal of Gerontology (Medical Sciences)*, 55A M400 -M405.

Koenig, H.G.; George, L.K.; Meador, K.G.; Blazer, D.G. & Ford, S.M. "Religious Coping and Depression in Elderly Medically Hospitalized Men," *American Journal of Psychiatry*, 149, 1963 - 1700.

Koenig, H.G.; George, L.K.; Peterson, B.L.; "Religiosity and Remission of Depression in Medically Ill Older Patients." *American Journal of Psychiatry*, 155(4), 336. 1998.

The Ages Digital Library Theology. "The Master Christian Library, Version 8," Ages Software, Inc. Wisconsin.

A Journey With a Future

OBJECTIVES

- Demonstrate the use of poetry to express inner emotions and true feelings
- Use of poetry to express victories in trials and in tribulations.

A Journey With a Future

OBJECTIVES

- Demonstrate the use of poetry to express inner emotions and true feelings
- Use of poetry to express victories in trials and in tribulations.

COMFORT
© Brenda S. Jackson

Comfort to me Lord You are.

Taking away the pain of sorrow,

You remind me that You bring the tomorrows.

Wiping away my tears of sadness,

With Your Word You give me strokes of gladness.

Memories of Love, You gave me to treasure,

While burying the recollections which do not bring pleasure.

Thank You Lord for being my comfort.

"My Hope"

© Brenda Simuel Jackson

Hope was born in me.
Hope is my eternity.
Hope guides me each day.
It is hope that lets me see my way.
Hope brings joy in times of struggle,
Hope allows rest even when there is trouble.
Jesus, the Christ, is all the hope I need.
Jesus, the Christ is my Hope in deed.
The Holy Spirit keeps me in tune with my hope,
The Holy Spirit never lets hope drain, and never leaves me to grope.

I AM MORTAL
© Brenda Simuel Jackson

I am mortal, born to die.

I am mortal, body decay is a sign of life.

I am mortal, strength decreases lagging behind my will.

I am mortal, information once gained, I don't always retain.

I am mortal, mortality has lessened my number of friends.

I am mortal, but my future is not grim.

I am mortal, but I have my security deposit for eternal life.

I am mortal, departed friends and family, one day I know I will see.

I am mortal, with everlasting life with Christ is my guarantee.

I am mortal, but that's Okay, Immortality is a gift Christ has given to me.

MANAGING THE PAIN
© Brenda Simuel Jackson

The left side, down the thigh and sometimes the leg goes the pain, occasionally making a visit to the right.

Bending over or down causes grimaces of pain, getting up in the morning bring cries of Lord help.

Pills bring short time relief by dulling the sharpness, and the anguish of this enemy, this trouble, called pain.

Remembering the song, I will Trust in The Lord, takes my mental focus away from my discomfort, I remember Your word that says You will never leave me or forsake me, and as I go through rivers of pain, they will not sweep over me.

I remember the pharmacy in the hem of Your garment which brings me joy, I remember my weeping may endure for the night, but there is expectant joy in the morning.

I cried out, and You heard, and enabled me to rise, to walk, to carry, to sit, to travel, to endure, for now the pain is eased, and I can continue one episode at a time.

Thank You!

GOD'S GRACE
© Brenda Simuel Jackson

1967-1992

Businesses were burning, gun shots were ringing clear.
Couldn't go to Church that Sunday evening, but
God's Grace was near.

A happy day, the day I wed, and changed my regular bed.
A day of God's Grace,
A day of His shining face.

Work by Day, School by night,
A spouse with problems, were part of my plight
With each obstacle presented, by
God's Grace I have never lamented.

My father answered his call,
My brother rushed his life with a fall.
My Dear mother fought the good fight,
and by God's Grace, all are spiritually alright.

I know not if my spouse, I will again see,
but by the Grace of God,
I know where I shall be.

DIFFERENCES, DO THEY MATTER?
© Brenda Simuel Jackson

Does it Matter that we are different?
I am Black and you are not.
I am old and you are young.
Does it really Matter that we are different?
I have degrees, and you have one.
Does it Matter truly, that we are different?
I was born in the mid-west, you in the South;
Does it matter that you can walk and I can't,
I can hear, and you don't.
Does it matter, I am rich in Spirit, you in silver and gold?
Does it make a difference?

Only if we look from a different point of view.

HEY CHAPLAIN
© Brenda Simuel Jackson

Hey Chaplain didn't get that visit requested.
Hey Chaplain can't read the print in the KJV bequested.
Hey Chaplain, who appointed you for the Lord and Master?
Hey Chaplain, will you mail this letter faster?
Hey Chaplain when will my cup run over?
Hey Chaplain, guess what, my prayers are getting louder and bolder!
Hey Chaplain, I didn't cry last night.
I got a visit from Jesus, and not by my might!
Hey Chaplain, thanks again for helping me to see, I have a friend in Jesus,
He loves me!
Hey Chaplain!

THE CHURCH, MORE THAN A BUILDING
© Brenda Simuel Jackson

More than a building is The Church

An organism not held together with bricks and steel is The Church,

Not just a place to greet, meet, and eat is The Church, but

A living building with Jesus as the cornerstone is The Church.

Built with Called Out Believers, fitted together with Christ, is The Church,

Filled with serving, worshipping, and doing His Will is The Church,

Praying together in faith, with unity in praise is The Church,

Yes,

More than a building is The Church, a People called out from the World, belonging to Christ, is The Church.

"Graduation Day for the Incarcerated of Camp Brighton"

© Brenda Simuel Jackson

It is Graduation Day.
This is the start of a new life.
It is Graduation Day,
I thank You, Lord for each class of trials You helped me successfully pass.
It is Graduation Day,
I look forward to a future of no crime or shame.
It is Graduation Day,
I can hold my head high, and reach for the sky.
It is Graduation Day;
I know I will never be alone.
It is Graduation Day;
I will find a new home.
It is Graduation Day;
I thank my Lord, each officer, and inmate who helped me overcome.
It is Graduation Day;
This is my second start.
I thank You Lord, for this my Graduation Day.

BRENDA S. JACKSON, Ph.D

Brenda Simuel Jackson (BA, MA, Master of Divinity, Ph.D.), is a born again Christian, affiliated with the Baptist Faith. She is a member and Minister of New Prospect Missionary Baptist Church, and does ministry through BSJ Christian Seminars, a Prison/Jail Ministry, and an outreach and equipment ministry. She is a graduate of Wayne State University, and Michigan Theological Seminary. As a member of the Pulpit Ministry, she assists in the teaching, prison ministries and intercessory prayer ministry of New Prospect Baptist Church in Detroit, MI.

Dr. Jackson has over thirty years of experience in human services, education administration, and management, as well as part-time collegiate instruction. She is currently a part-time faculty member of Wayne County Community College District. She has presented at Conferences of the American Association of Christian Counselors, local church women's retreats, mission programs, Christian Education Institutes, State Correctional Facilities, as well as Professional and Community Programs.

Dr. Jackson is also a published writer and has hosted a radio broadcast, "God's Teaching Moment". Her Christian Journey includes short term outreach mission assignments in Japan, South Africa, and Jamaica. Her goals include future short term missions.

A native Detroiter, Dr. Jackson is a widow, a mother, a grandmother, and the ninth child of Willie and Lucy Simuel (both deceased). Dr. Jackson is a called minister of the Gospel, and was endorsed for Chaplaincy clergy by the National Baptist Convention, USA, Inc. Home Mission Board in June 2004.

She is a certified teacher for the Sunday School Publishing Board. Dr. Jackson has been licensed as a minister of the gospel since November 13, 2005. Her vineyard is the prisons of the world.

For more information or to contact Dr. Jackson, write or call:

BSJ Christian Seminars
P.O. Box 21004
Detroit, MI 48221
(313) 550-0081

Or visit on the World Wide Web at:
www.bsjchristianseminars.org

BOOK ORDER FORM

Reflections on the Path to Wholeness: A Journey of Redeeming Faith
By Brenda S. Jackson, Ph.D.

Name _____

Address _____

City _____ State _____ Zip _____

Phone _____ Fax _____

Email _____

Quantity	
Price *(each)*	$9.99
Subtotal	
S & H *(each)*	$1.99
MI Tax 6%	
TOTAL	

METHOD OF PAYMENT:

☐ Check or Money Order (*Make payable to*: **PriorityONE Publications**)

☐ Visa ☐ Master Card ☐ American Express

Acct No. _____

Expiration Date (*mmyy*) _____

Signature _____

Mail your payment with this form to:
PriorityONE Publications
P. O. Box 725
Farmington, MI 48332
(800) 331-8841 – Toll Free
(313) 893-3359 – Southeast Michigan
URL: http://www.p1pubs.com
Email: info@p1pubs.com

Notes

www.ingramcontent.com/pod-product-compliance
Lightning Source LLC
Chambersburg PA
CBHW052058070526
44584CB00017B/2240